CHECKERBOARD BIOGRAPHY LIBRARY

EXPLORERS

Marco Polo

Kristin Petrie

ABDO
Publishing Company

visit us at
www.abdopublishing.com

Published by ABDO Publishing Company, 4940 Viking Drive, Edina, Minnesota 55435.
Copyright © 2007 by Abdo Consulting Group, Inc. International copyrights reserved in all
countries. No part of this book may be reproduced in any form without written permission from
the publisher. The Checkerboard Library™ is a trademark and logo of ABDO Publishing
Company.

Printed in the United States.

Cover Photos: Corbis
Interior Photos: Bridgeman Art Library pp. 21, 25; Corbis pp. 9, 13, 23, 27; Getty Images pp. 5,
    15, 29; North Wind pp. 7, 11, 17

Series Coordinator: Heidi M. Dahmes
Editors: Rochelle Baltzer, Heidi M. Dahmes
Art Direction & Cover Design: Neil Klinepier
Interior Design & Maps: Dave Bullen

Library of Congress Cataloging-in-Publication Data

Petrie, Kristin, 1970-
 Marco Polo / Kristin Petrie.
    p. cm. -- (Explorers)
 Includes index.
 ISBN-10 1-59679-747-9
 ISBN-13 978-1-59679-747-5
 1. Polo, Marco, 1254-1323?--Juvenile literature. 2. Explorers--Italy--Biography--Juvenile
literature. 3. Travel, Medieval--Juvenile literature. I. Title II. Series: Petrie, Kristin, 1970- .
Explorers.

G370.P9P48 2006
915.042'2'092--dc22
                                                                    2005017501

J
92
Polo, M.

Contents

Marco Polo

Marco Polo was an explorer ahead of his time. This courageous traveler was the first European to cross the entire continent of Asia. More important, he left a record of what he saw and heard on his journeys.

When he was just a teenager, Polo traveled to present-day China. There, he made friends with the emperor. And, Polo served as one of his ambassadors. As an ambassador, Polo traveled throughout the **Far East**. In this way, he became familiar with various peoples and **cultures**.

Later in life, Polo wrote a book about his journeys. *Description of the World* introduced Europeans to foreign countries. However, many people believe that Polo elaborated the details of his observations. Nevertheless, Polo's descriptions of faraway places became of great interest to the Europeans.

1271
Polo left for Asia

1295
Polo returned to Italy

1254
Marco Polo born

1275
Polo met Kublai Khan

There is a famous story about Marco Polo. It states that while on his deathbed, he was asked to take back the "fables" he had made up in his book. In response Polo declared, "I did not write half of what I saw."

1460 or 1474
Juan Ponce de León born

1480
Ferdinand Magellan born

1324
Polo died

1475
Vasco Núñez de Balboa born

Early Years

Marco Polo was born in the lively seaport city of Venice, Italy. His birth date is uncertain, but it was sometime in the year 1254. Marco was born into a wealthy family of merchants.

In 1255 Marco's father, Niccolò, traveled to the **Far East**. Niccolò and his brother Maffeo sailed from Venice to Constantinople. This city was a main trading center between eastern and western countries. From there, the men continued on to Cathay, or present-day northern China.

During his father's absence, Marco's mother died. Marco was an only child, so an aunt and uncle raised him. They trained him to be a merchant. So, he learned how to use foreign money, judge products, and handle cargo ships. Marco also studied reading, writing, and arithmetic.

1500
Balboa joined expedition to South America

1493
Ponce de León joined expedition to New World

1502
Ponce de León became governor of Higüey

Would You?

Would you enjoy studying to be a merchant? Do you think Polo's lessons were tough? What else do you think a merchant would need to know?

1508
Ponce de León's first expedition

1514
Ponce de León knighted by King Ferdinand II

1513
Ponce de León's second expedition, found Florida and the Gulf Stream; Balboa was the first European to sight the Pacific Ocean

Young Marco

In Venice, the trade between people of various **cultures** influenced Marco. He heard tales of faraway places while wandering through the port's streets. Naturally, the young man wondered in what distant land his father might be.

To the Polo family's surprise, Niccolò and Maffeo returned to Venice in 1269. Marco was 15 years old and entranced by his father's stories of adventure. The men had traveled through Asia. They met people from many cultures, including Kublai **Khan**. The emperor asked that upon their return to Italy, the brothers be his ambassadors to the pope.

After two years back home, Niccolò and Maffeo were eager to return to the East. This time, they decided 17-year-old Marco would join them. Marco was a bright young man and would be very helpful on their journey.

1520
Magellan discovered the Strait of Magellan

1554
Walter Raleigh born

1519
Magellan led expedition to Spice Islands; Balboa died

1521
Ponce de León's third expedition, died in Cuba; Magellan died

Would You?

Would you be excited about traveling to an entirely different continent? Where would you want to travel? Do you think Polo was nervous to leave Venice? What do you think he took with him?

While living in Venice, Marco learned many things that would prepare him for the Far East.

New Adventure

In 1271, Marco, Niccolò, and Maffeo set sail in the Mediterranean Sea. The trio headed south for the port of Acre. From there, the men visited the sacred city of Jerusalem. They obtained oil from the Holy **Sepulchre** of Christ, as requested by the **khan**.

That same year, a new pope was elected. Pope Gregory X sent the Polos on their way with gifts for the khan. He also sent two friars to accompany the Polos on their journey.

Once assembled, the small group sailed on to the seaport of Ayas, now Yumurtalik, Turkey. When they reached Armenia, they received news of war. The friars turned back in fear, but the Polos traveled on.

While crossing present-day Iraq and Iran, bandits attacked the men. Marco, Niccolò, and Maffeo escaped without harm. But, they also faced harsh conditions. They traversed freezing mountains and hot deserts. Finally, they arrived in the city of Hormuz on the Persian Gulf.

1580
John Smith born

1585
Raleigh knighted by Queen Elizabeth I

1565
Henry Hudson born

1584–1589
Raleigh sponsored expeditions

Would You?

Would you be tempted to return home after hearing about war or facing bandits? Do you think Polo ever asked to turn back?

Traveling On

Marco, Niccolò, and Maffeo had hoped to reach China by ship. But after seeing the unsafe boats, they made another tough decision. The men continued their journey by land.

Heading north, the men soon reached the region of Badakhshan in Afghanistan. The Polos remained there for about a year. Historians believe they were delayed by illness. During this time, Marco may have journeyed to southern lands such as Pakistan and Kashmir.

Leaving Badakhshan, Marco, Niccolò, and Maffeo continued east to the Pamirs. They crossed peaks that stood between 13,000 and 15,000 feet (4,000 and 5,000 m) above sea level. Marco marveled at the large sheep that lived there. To this day, they are known as Marco Polo sheep.

As the Polos passed through Silk Road cities, they prepared for their biggest challenge yet. The Gobi Desert

1595
Raleigh led first expedition

1588
Raleigh helped defeat the Spanish Armada

1606
Smith joined expedition to North America

lay before them. At the **oasis** of Lop Nur, the men rested and ate. Other than what they could carry, there would be no food for an entire month.

The Silk Road was an ancient trade route that linked China to the West. Silk traveled from the East. Wools, gold, and silver came from the West by camel caravan.

New Sights

As the Polos crossed the Gobi Desert, the sun beat down on them. In his book, Marco states that they saw neither "beast nor bird" in the Gobi. After 30 days, they reached the city of Shazhou, today known as Dunhuang.

After a short rest, the Polos continued east. As they traveled farther into China, Marco recorded many new sights. He noted large, woolly beasts called yaks. And, delicate gazelle-like creatures bounded about. These animals were hunted for musk.

The Tatar people were especially interesting to Marco. He learned about their **nomadic** lifestyle. These people moved from the mountains to the plains in different seasons. The men and women worked together to clothe, feed, and protect each other. They fought fiercely in times of war.

Continuing on, a team of escorts greeted the weary travelers in 1275. Kublai **Khan** had heard of their approach.

1607
Hudson's first expedition

1609
Hudson's third expedition

1608
Hudson's second expedition

Kublai Khan was emperor of China's Yüan, or Mongol, dynasty.

Under the care of the escorts, the Polos were well fed and cared for. Soon, they reached the **Mongol** summer capital of Shangdu.

1614
Smith led expedition to North America, charted and named New England

1610-1611
Hudson's last expedition, he died

1616
Raleigh's second expedition

Life in Cathay

The **khan** was thrilled to see Niccolò and Maffeo. Marco was introduced and welcomed as warmly as his father and his uncle. The Polos presented the emperor with the gifts and letters from the pope. The ruler was especially pleased with the holy oil. The three travelers were treated to an elaborate celebration.

During his stay with the khan, Marco learned many things. The paper money the people of Cathay used impressed him. Back in Europe, money was in the form of heavy gold, copper, or lead coins.

Marco also learned many differences between European and Cathayan **culture**. For example, the people of Cathay mined and used coal as fuel. Coal had not yet been used in Europe. Marco called coal "black stones."

Even more impressive to Marco was the Cathayan postal system. This system consisted of a number of stations.

1618
Raleigh died

1637
Jacques Marquette born

1645
Louis Jolliet born

1631
Smith died

1643
René-Robert Cavelier de La Salle born

People called messengers ran or rode horseback with letters and packages for the emperor. Distant information could be delivered in two days and two nights! Normally it would have taken at least ten days to receive information.

Kublai Khan warmly welcomed his long-awaited visitors.

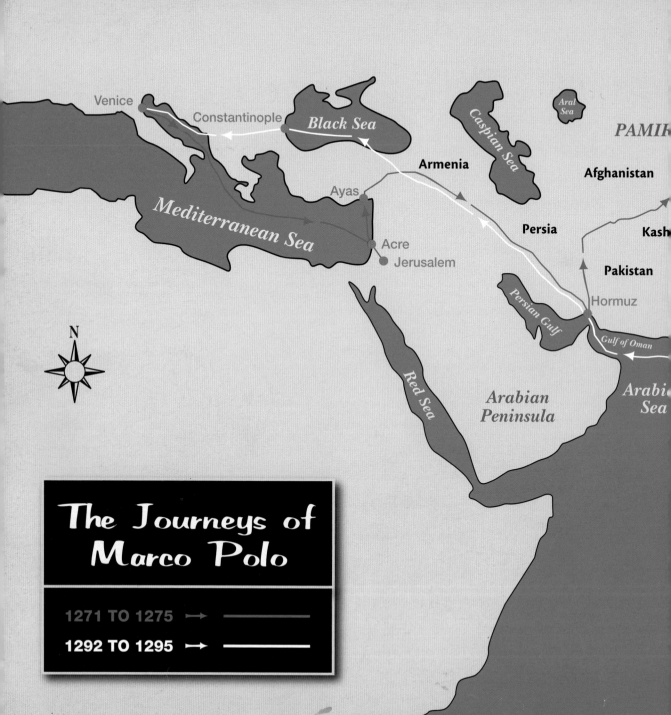

Venice

Constantinople

Black Sea

Aral Sea

PAMIR

Caspian Sea

Armenia

Afghanistan

Ayas

Mediterranean Sea

Persia

Kash

Acre

Jerusalem

Persian Gulf

Pakistan

Hormuz

Gulf of Oman

Red Sea

Arabian Peninsula

Arabi Sea

N

The Journeys of Marco Polo

1271 TO 1275 ➞ ━━━━━━

1292 TO 1295 ➞ ━━━━━━

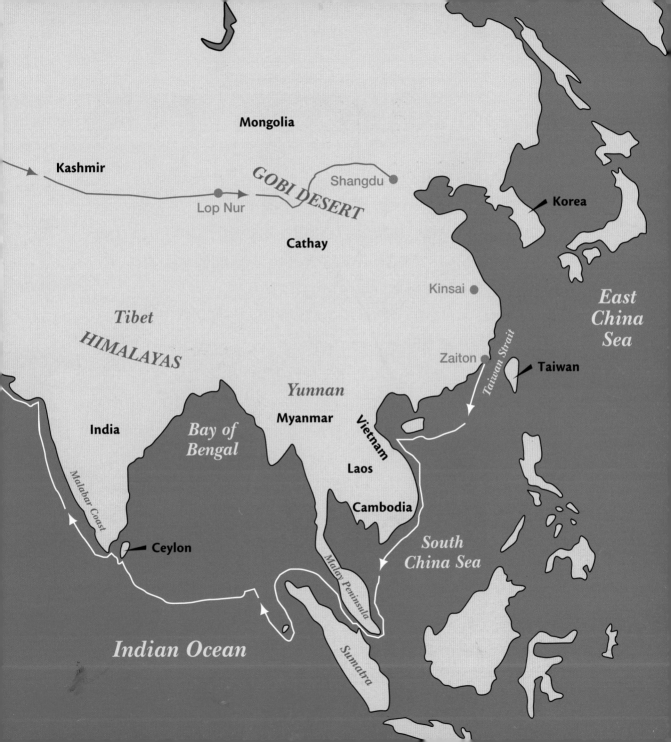

Ambassador

Kublai **Khan** thought highly of Polo. The young man knew four languages. He had an amazing memory and communicated well. Polo agreed to become the emperor's ambassador. Soon, he began traveling to distant parts of the khan's empire on fact-finding missions.

The khan's empire did not just include today's China. It also encompassed present-day Mongolia, Cambodia, Korea, and Myanmar. With such a vast region to rule, the khan relied on ambassadors to travel and gather information for him.

Polo went on a four-month journey to the west for the khan. He eventually reached the **province** of Tibet. Years of war had destroyed the cities there. The people lived by hunting animals and gathering fruits. Travelers in the area had to protect themselves from roaming lions, bears, and lynx.

1669
La Salle explored Ohio region

1666
La Salle sailed to Canada

1673
Marquette and Jolliet explored the Mississippi River

Polo saw many wonders, such as these towers in Myanmar, on his journeys.

Continuing on, the ambassador reached Yunnan in southwestern China. **Mongols** had recently conquered this **province**. One of the **khan**'s grandsons ruled Yunnan.

Polo eventually reached present-day Myanmar. In the capital city, Polo noted two beautiful towers. One of these towers was plated in gold, the other in silver. The towers stood over a past king's tomb.

Another assignment took Polo to southeastern China. There, he visited the city of Kinsai, today known as Hangzhou. Polo felt Kinsai was a magnificent city. Citizens dressed in fine silk. And, grand houses with gardens lined the streets. Polo probably didn't want to leave this heavenly city!

Polo's work as the **khan**'s ambassador may have taken him even farther. Polo claims to have made the long sea voyage to Sri Lanka. Back then, this island was called Ceylon. It was not part of the khan's empire. Nevertheless, the khan had a strong interest in other **cultures** and religions.

Polo did not sail back to China when his work on Ceylon was complete. Instead, he turned his **fleet** north and reached India. On the country's eastern coast, Polo learned about the leading industry, pearl fishing.

Next, Polo sailed around the base of India and up the Malabar Coast. Polo learned much about the **Hindu** religion. He remained in India for some time and learned about its people, culture, and **customs**.

1675
Marquette died

1682
La Salle's second Mississippi River expedition

1679
La Salle's first Mississippi River expedition

When Polo visited Kinsai, the city had an estimated population of 1 to 1.5 million people.

During Polo's 17 years of service to the **khan**, he had many amazing experiences. He traveled the Taiwan Strait and visited present-day Myanmar, Laos, Vietnam, and India. Polo watched as Kublai Khan's empire prospered. He also benefited from the khan's success. Polo was wealthy beyond his dreams.

1687
La Salle died

1684
La Salle's third Mississippi River expedition

1700
Jolliet died

Royal Journey

The Polos lived a good life in China. However, in time they began thinking about their family in Venice. The men also worried about their safety in China. Kublai **Khan** was almost 80 years old. If he died, it could be dangerous for the Polos. Because the khan had treated them so well, they had gained jealous rivals.

Marco, Niccolò, and Maffeo asked for permission to return to Venice. But, the emperor did not want them to leave. Luckily, a change came when Arghun Khan of Persia made a special request. The Persian ruler asked Kublai Khan to send a **Mongol** princess to be his bride.

The Polos seized this opportunity. They offered to accompany the princess on this journey. The khan was heartbroken to see them leave, but he agreed to the proposal. The Polos were eager to leave China. They planned to return to Venice after their journey with the princess.

1770
William Clark born

1786
Sacagawea born

1774
Meriwether Lewis born

1800
Sacagawea captured

Would You?

Would you be excited to return to a city that you hadn't seen in more than 20 years? What do you think Polo expected to find when he returned to Venice?

Return Home

A **fleet** of 14 ships was assembled to transport the royal wedding party. The Polos joined about 600 sailors, soldiers, and **courtiers** for the journey. Around 1292, the ships set sail from China's southern port of Zaiton, today known as Quanzhou.

The fleet stopped at modern-day Vietnam, as well as several islands and the Malay **Peninsula**. **Monsoon** season forced the ships to stop on the island of Sumatra for five months.

Finally, the escort party reached the port of Hormuz. The expedition continued to lead the young princess inland to Khorasan. This was where she was to meet her future husband.

Marco, Niccolò, and Maffeo delivered the princess and eventually left Khorasan to return to Europe. The overland journey was difficult and dangerous.

1804
Lewis and Clark began exploring the Pacific Northwest

1806
Lewis and Clark returned to Missouri

1805
Sacagawea joined the Lewis and Clark expedition

By the time the expedition reached Khorasan, Arghun Khan had died. So, the young princess married the khan's son instead.

Unfortunately, the Polos had no protection once they left **Mongol** lands. When they entered Christian territory in modern Turkey, they were robbed of most of their treasures. But, the hardy travelers pushed on and reached Venice in 1295.

1812
Sacagawea died

1856
Robert Edwin Peary born

1809
Lewis died

1838
Clark died

1881
Peary entered the U.S. Navy

Travel Writer

Marco, Niccolò, and Maffeo had been away from Venice for 24 years. According to legend, the weary men received an unpleasant welcome when they returned. After so much time without word from the travelers, relatives considered the men dead. Each man had to prove his own identity!

At the time of Polo's return, Venice was at war with the neighboring city of Genoa. During a battle at sea, the Genoese captured Polo and imprisoned him. During **captivity**, the seasoned traveler met writer Rustichello of Pisa. Together, they decided to put Polo's travel experiences in writing.

Polo **dictated** his adventures and memories to Rustichello. Polo gave detailed accounts of what he learned and saw during his time in Asia. The book was originally titled *Description of the World*. Polo's amazing memory and talent for description shines through in his stories.

1893
Peary's first expedition

1909
Peary's third expedition, reached the North Pole

1905
Peary's second expedition

1920
Peary died

Polo was released from prison in 1299 and returned to Venice. He married a woman named Donata, had three daughters, and continued to work in the trading business. Marco Polo died on January 8, 1324, but his writings inspired many explorers after him.

Polo told his extraordinary adventures while he was a Genoese prisoner.

Glossary

captivity - the state of being captured and held against one's will.

courtier - one in attendance at the home or court of a ruler.

culture - the customs, arts, and tools of a nation or people at a certain time.

custom - a habit of a group that is passed on through generations.

dictate - to speak or read for a person to record.

Far East - usually considered to consist of the Asian countries bordering on the Pacific Ocean.

fleet - a group of ships under one command.

Hinduism - a religion of India. It emphasizes dharma, or the principles of existence, and its rituals and ceremonies.

khan - any of the medieval emperors of China and rulers over the Turkish, Tatar, and Mongol tribes.

Mongol - a nomadic person from Mongolia.

monsoon - a seasonal wind that sometimes brings heavy rain. Monsoon season occurs during the summer months in the Indian Ocean and southern Asia.

nomad - a member of a tribe that moves from place to place.

oasis - a place in the desert with water, trees, and plants.

peninsula - land that sticks out into water and is connected to a larger landmass.

province - a geographical or governmental division of a country.

sepulchre - a burial place, such as a tomb.

Saying It

Badakhshan - bah-dahk-SHAHN
Cathay - kuh-THAY
Ceylon - suh-LAHN
Genoa - JEH-noh-uh
Hangzhou - HAHNG-JOH
Kinsai - KIHN-SAY
Kublai Khan - KOO-bluh KAHN
sepulchre - SEH-puhl-kuhr
Tatar - TAH-tuhr

Web Sites

To learn more about Marco Polo, visit ABDO Publishing Company on the World Wide Web at **www.abdopublishing.com**. Web sites about Polo are featured on our Book Links page. These links are routinely monitored and updated to provide the most current information available.

Index